THE GHATOTKACHA GAME

MARKETING LESSONS FROM MYTHOLOGY

I0479610

PRAVIN SHEKAR
& SHRADDHA ANU SHEKAR

INDIA · SINGAPORE · MALAYSIA

Notion Press

No.8, 3rd Cross Street
CIT Colony, Mylapore
Chennai, Tamil Nadu – 600004

First Published by Notion Press 2020
Copyright © Pravin Shekar & Shraddha Anu Shekar 2020
All Rights Reserved.

ISBN 978-1-64919-541-8

The Lineage of Ghatotkacha

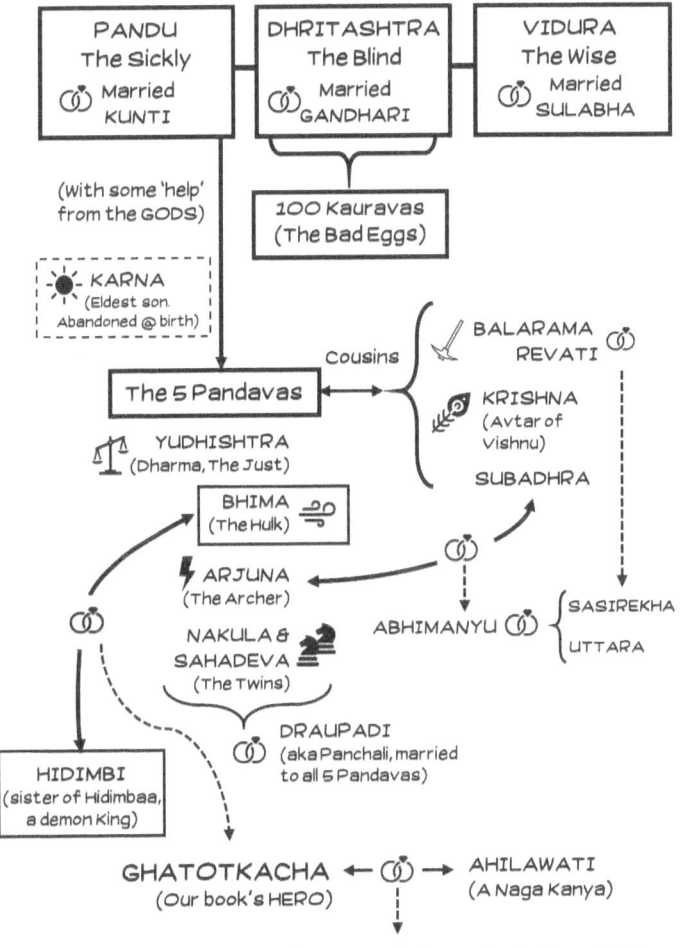

PANDU
The Sickly
💍 Married
KUNTI

DHRITASHTRA
The Blind
💍 Married
GANDHARI

VIDURA
The Wise
💍 Married
SULABHA

(with some 'help'
from the GODS)

100 Kauravas
(The Bad Eggs)

KARNA
(Eldest son.
Abandoned @ birth)

The 5 Pandavas

Cousins

BALARAMA
REVATI 💍

KRISHNA
(Avtar of
Vishnu)

SUBADHRA

YUDHISHTRA
(Dharma, The Just)

BHIMA
(The Hulk)

ARJUNA
(The Archer)

NAKULA &
SAHADEVA
(The Twins)

💍

ABHIMANYU 💍

SASIREKHA

UTTARA

💍

DRAUPADI
(aka Panchali, married
to all 5 Pandavas)

HIDIMBI
(sister of Hidimbaa,
a demon King)

GHATOTKACHA ← 💍 → AHILAWATI
(Our book's HERO)   (A Naga Kanya)

BELAARSEN | ANJANAPARVAN | MEGHAVARNA

💍 Spouse   ---► Offspring

Testimonial

"What a truly special book – beyond it being a father/daughter exercise – which is beautiful in itself. I love mythology, and Shraddha Anu Shekar has inspired me to dig deeper into Indian mythology. Her dad, Pravin Shekar, is a marvel in how he draws marketing conclusions from these famous stories. It is truly spectacular. A must-read for anyone in marketing or leading businesses."

Andrea T Edwards,
The Digital Conversationalist.

About the Authors

This is a father and daughter's first book together.

Shraddha Anu Shekar is a thirteen-year-old mythology enthusiast. She loves reading, writing and re-telling mythologies from different cultures. This is Shraddha Anu Shekar's fourth book. She calls herself "The Teen Mythologist" and searches for lesser known stories.

If you would like to share mythology stories, please write to me@shraddhaanushekar.com

www.ShraddhaAnuShekar.com

Other Books by Shraddha:

Shraddha Anu Shekar: www.ShraddhaAnuShekar. com/books

- SHALYA: Stories from the Mahabharata
- MURUGA: The god of war
- The adventures of Morty

* * * * *

Pravin Shekar is an Outlier marketer and a raconteur.

Unconventional marketing is his forte. When the world moves one way, you need to move another way: that's his philosophy. This going-against-the-grain attitude helps him find opportunity in every crisis.

A recipient of the American Marketing Association's "Emerging Leader" award. He is passionate about marketing and believes that micro marketing can redefine the business environment.

When you need to shake up your marketing strategy and re-gear your growth, reach out to him at mic@pravinshekar.com & www.linkedin.com/in/pravinshekar

Other Books by Pravin:

Pravin Shekar: www.pravinshekar.com/publishing

MARKETING

- DEVIL DOES CARE: Outlier Marketing for Bootstrapped Entrepreneurs

- HOW TO GET MY FIRST PAID SPEAKING GIG!

- VIRTUAL SUMMIT PLAYBOOK: A Guide to Hosting Your Own Online Conference.

- CLIMB YOUR WAY OUT OF HELL: Outlier Marketing to Overcome Worst-case Scenarios and Grow Your Business

- THE GHATOTKACHA GAME: Marketing Lessons from Mythology *(yes, the book you are reading!)*

TALK-BOOK

- OPHTHALMOLOGISTS BRAND YOURSELF!

CREATIVITY

- WITH YOU, FOR YOU: A Collection of Travel Images and Romantic Poems

IN THE PIPELINE

- LOVE IS JUST A PAGE AWAY: Short Stories from the Heart

- STREET SMART MARKETING: Marketing Lessons from the Street Vendors of Chennai

Table of Contents

MAYABAZAAR

Marketing Lessons from Mythology

Are there any? Would it be a stretch to connect the dots, to learn from stories of yore, from characters that have been chiselled and enhanced across centuries?

There's only one way to find out. As Shraddha and I worked on *The Ghatotkacha Game*, I let my thoughts run amok and the same can be seen in the connections I have made.

My primary audience is me. What can I learn? What can I implement? What can I share? This is what comprises the running commentary along with the mythological stories.

To me, this is a marketing book enhanced by mythological characters and situational references. When I read a story or dig deeper into the definition of a character, I find nuggets that go into my marketing commonplace book.

The parallels I draw are my own, based on two decades of marketing various services, products and solutions.

I believe and evangelize that each of us, first and foremost, is a marketer. This hidden facet has to be brought to the front and in unusual ways. This exercise is one of them.

Marketing lessons in mythology and the many messages therein.

PRAVIN SHEKAR
Outlier Marketer

What is the Ghatotkacha Game?

Ghatotkacha is a compelling character in Indian mythology.

Everything from Ghatotkacha's birth to his death is a game. Does he play different games, or is he a part of one himself? One might say that Ghatotkacha played different games and played each one in his favour.

Others can argue saying that the *Mahabharata* was a game in itself and that Ghatotkacha was only a pawn in it.

The actual answer to that question, which may vary, lies in the mind of the person reading it.

After reading this book, ask yourself: did he play games or did he participate in the success of a bigger game? The answer that you get is neither right nor wrong. The correct answer depends on your perspective.

So go on, find your answer.

SHRADDHA ANU SHEKAR
The Teen Mythologist

Thanks to:

Viji Hari, Cathy Johnson, Andrea T Edwards, Jayashree Venkat, Ravi Venkataramani, Srijata Bhatnagar, TNC Venkatarangan.

Cover design and images: Arun Ramkumar from @ MojoCanvas

Naveen, Swetha and the NotionPress team.

To our family and friends.

The Asuri and the Prince

The Pandavas were in their period of exile of 13 years. The Kauravas had recently tried to kill them by burning them in a lac palace but failed to do so. The Pandavas, along with their widowed mother, went into hiding in the forests. This was when they stumbled upon the domain of an *asura* (demon) called Hidimbaa. As they were weary from travelling so far on foot, they decided to rest under the trees. Bheema, the strongest brother, decided to keep watch over his family.

A little distance away, Hidimbaa said to his sister, the *asuri* (demoness) Hidimbi*:

"Hidimbi, it has been many years since humans have entered this part of the forest. Go and bring them here under the impression of providing shelter. Once you do so, we will celebrate with a feast."

Hidimbi agreed with her brother and set out. She is said to have wielded powers that allowed her to transform

---

*   Hidimbi is also sometimes called Hadimba or Hidimba

herself. She is described as being ugly, a trait of an *asuri*. She transformed herself to look like an *apsara* (divine woman) and set out in search of the humans.

She reached the scene where the brothers were sleeping. Seeing Bheema being the only one awake, she started to talk to him. "I am Hidimbi. It is quite cold out here during the night. My brother asked me to search for any passersby. If there were any, he asked me to convey to them that he wishes for them to spend the night with us at our house."

Bheema did not turn around to acknowledge her presence. "I thank your brother for his generous offer, but I am to stay awake and look after my family." Saying so, Bheema went back to looking for any threat.

Hidimbi was disappointed by Bheema's reaction. Especially since no one had turned down her requests before, she decided to try again. "Listen, there are many wild animals around this area. It would be for the best if you would come and stay at our house."

Bheema turned around to face Hidimbi. "If there are wild animals around, it is of more importance that I stay with my family. You should also go back to your house and thank your brother for me." Saying so, Bheema continued not to pay her any attention. Hidimbi was impressed by Bheema's loyalty and also liked his courage. She did not want to kill him and decided to tell Bheema the truth.

"My actual name is Hidimbi, but I am an *asuri*." Hidimbi proceeded to reveal her true self to Bheema. Bheema was taken aback at the sight of her face. He almost attacked her before she started to explain herself. "My brother is the *asura* Hidimbaa, who governs this area. He ordered me to bring you to our abode so that we could eat you. But after seeing your loyalty towards your family, I decided not to kill you. I will offer you protection from my brother."

Hearing Hidimbi, Bheema became angry. But heeding her words, he waited for her brother to come to them.

Meanwhile, Hidimbaa grew impatient and worried that Hidimbi might have gotten into trouble. Finally, when she did not turn up even at the crack of dawn, Hidimbaa decided to go in search of his sister. When he found her with the Pandavas, he went ballistic. Hidimbi tried to protect the Pandavas, but Hidimbaa knew all her tricks.

Bheema got annoyed that Hidimbaa had come in search of them. When Hidimbaa tried to attack them, Bheema uprooted one of the trees nearby and hurled it at him. Hidimbaa responded by imitating Bheema's moves. Finally, when they had cleared most of the trees in the area, they began to wrestle. Bheema was a natural at wrestling since childhood. He easily defeated Hidimbaa and killed him by strangling him.

By this time, the Pandavas and their mother, Kunti, had woken up due to the commotion. They were initially shocked and scared for Bheema but were soon relieved. It was then that Hidimbi went to Kunti and requested for her consent to marry Bheema.

Kunti was taken aback by the sudden request, that too from an *asuri*, but agreed. "Hidimbi, I have a condition if you want to marry Bheema. You must only spend the days with him. He must be with us by nightfall. Also, after having a child, you must take the child and go back to the forest. Bheema cannot be seen with an *asuri* for a wife."

Hidimbi agreed with Kunti's condition, and she was married to Bheema.

MARKETING: Alliances and Partnerships

Alliances. They happen in the unlikeliest of places. At times, they are highly improbable, appearing doomed for failure.

Traditional alliances have commonalities, a strategic fit into a familiar framework. This makes it easy to understand and digest. It makes sense. There are corporate marriages that also take place which do not make any sense. What is their purpose? Is it only for shock value? That is unlikely, as the top management has a fiscal responsibility to their respective shareholders.

Is it a merger, an acquisition or a partnership?

Are we to look at alliances as short-term or long-term? Is the alliance merely an affair to achieve a single purpose in a short time window, or something longer? Are we looking at every new opportunity as an *apsara* (beauty) that we see? Or do we look beneath the beauty to see the reality? Do we get into the reality despite the ugliness or bare truth?

Go beyond linear thinking.

A new place, a new landscape and a new species too! Bheema partnered with someone who was sent to kill and eat him! Humans and *asuras* existed on different planes, never to co-exist. The thought itself may not have occurred to mere mortals.

Linear thinking would have ensured that Bhima killed the siblings right there and moved on. Yet when the opportunity presented itself, Bhima took it on.

Was Bheema thinking about the future and all the support he would need? Was he planning for the future and building his support base?

Was this then an alliance only to sow his seeds, literally speaking?

Astute collaboration is the hallmark of a marketer.

As Seth Godin says, "There are no original ideas, only original combinations."

A human–asura combination is definitely an original combination, which served the purpose manifold, as we will read on.

What are your business growth plans? And who figures in it? Who can help further your growth?

What outlier alliances should you work on?

Let's look at some real-life examples to propel your thought process:

BMW and Louis Vuitton

What does a luxury carmaker have to do with a luxury bag maker?

Let us look at the consumer. The typical BMW customer wants the best in design and luxury. The car is a showpiece symbol that reflects him/her. The customer is ready to pay a premium for the overt and subconscious reactions that are associated with BMW – class, quality design, perfection and quality service.

Isn't that similar to the wants of a customer of Louis Vuitton? For their new sports car, the BMW i8, BMW entered into a partnership with Louis Vuitton (LV). LV designed an exclusive 4-piece set of suitcases that were a perfect fit for the car's boot!

Patients As a Part of the Strategic Team

Yes! UCB, a pharmaceutical company, communicated directly with sets of patients with specific diseases. These patient sets received marketing messages along with information on their disease, associated treatments and newer explorations. These sets then worked with UCB to help strategies and innovate newer products.

* * * * *

WIELD THE MACE:

Which non-competing companies are providing solutions to the same clientele as yours? What is the mutual value-add by partnering?

When and how will you approach them?

The Giant Baby

Hidimbi was travelling with the five Pandavas and Mother Kunti through the forest. She had assumed the form of the *apsara* maiden. Hidimbi, knowing the entire forest, showed Bheema several places filled with magic. "Look there! Those two trees are gateways to a secret cave where my mother taught me how to use my magic. My mother also learned magic from her mother here. From the outside, they look ordinary, apart from their crookedness. But they are actually like a doorway." Bheema smiled, looking at his wife's excitement.

A month later, Hidimbi was pregnant. Kunti helped her, and so did Bheema. He pressed her feet and brought her sweet fruits from the trees. Bheema carried her as they continued their journey. His four brothers often joked around, saying that Bheema had transformed from a brave lion to a gentle, tamed cat.

Soon the weather changed as it was the heavy monsoon, and the family camped at different spots every few days. Kunti, who was still not over the fact that her son had married an *asuri*, said that the rain was a forecast of doom. As they walked through the forest, many animals and birds helped the Pandavas. As a result, the entire forest heard about Hidimbi and Bheema. When they heard that their first child was going to be born, all gathered round to view the birth of the child. The rain was now falling gently.

Deer, lions, tigers, bears, rabbits, sparrows and even dragonflies attended the celebration. Even Krishna*, an incarnation of Lord Vishnu, stood in silence. The onlookers and the Pandavas waited in anticipation. They heard a loud cry. The rain stopped almost immediately.

The brothers smiled in joy and congratulated Bheema. Hidimbi signalled Bheema to come into the tent. She showed Bheema the first son of the Pandavas. Bheema's eyes stung with tears. He held the baby carefully in his arms. He brought the baby out of the tent just as the first few rays of sunlight appeared.

Bheema came out of the tent holding the baby in his hands. When he came into the light, the baby transformed into a grown giant! The giant bellowed. The animals cried and ran away, leaving the grassy ground almost grassless. The onlooking men and women shrieked and prepared to attack the monster. Bheema felt lightheaded. *Was he dreaming?*

---

*   Krishna was a cousin of the Pandavas

Kunti went into the tent without saying a word. Hidimbi took a rock in her hands and closed her eyes. She expected her child to have powers, but even she did not know what magic this was. The brothers had their weapons out, but the giant did nothing. Bheema paid no attention to his brothers and stared at the giant with glassy eyes. The remaining brothers wondered if they should attack the giant or leave him alone.

The giant was grey (some stories say that he had normal human skin) and buff. He had pointy ears, was bald and wore a green loincloth with gold bordering around his waist. He wore accessories matching his dress, such as big gold earrings and bracelets. His teeth were blinding white, and he had long fangs, like those of a vampire. He stood still and was staring into the sky for a while. The giant finally moved. He turned around to face the brothers and Hidimbi.

Bheema's four brothers stood in anxiety. *Would the giant cause harm?* The giant looked around at all the brothers and stopped at Bheema. He knelt when Arjuna unleashed an arrow. The giant, if he felt any pain at all, did not show it. He prostrated to Bheema and then to Hidimbi. Bheema stared in astonishment at the giant baby. The initial fear of the giant had gone, but the brothers were still wary of him. Kunti and Draupadi had come to the door of the tent holding pitchers.

Bheema signalled Hidimbi to come closer. "What do we name him?" he whispered, still not used to the giant.

"I'm not sure. What about Ghatotkacha?" Bheema thought for a while. As he was about to speak, Kunti intervened. "It does seem like a good name. After all, Ghatam means pot and Utkacham means... well, bald." Kunti smiled.

"Well then, I don't think that anybody opposes the name." Bheema turned to the giant. "We will henceforth call you Ghatotkacha. Do you have an objection to the name?" Ghatotkacha shook his head. Bheema now looked at Ghatotkacha with admiration. "Son, I bless you that you will always excel at whatever you do." Ghatotkacha cracked a smile, that looked more sinister than a smile of happiness.

It was only then that Krishna came into the picture. He had been standing quietly and observing the scene going on. "Pandavas! I am very pleased to have heard the news about the child's birth in advance. Ghatotkacha, I am one of your uncles. My, you look healthy! Must have been the wild berries. Anyways, I am here to bless you."

Krishna cleared his throat. "Your strength will be unbeatable. You shall only lose a battle to one that is worthy of defeating you." Saying so, Krishna disappeared.

Kunti spoke up. "Hidimbi, have you forgotten our condition?" Hidimbi looked at Bheema and Kunti, startled. She had forgotten about the condition. She looked at Bheema crestfallen.

"Very well, I suppose that I should be going. Come Ghatotkacha, let us prostrate to Mother Kunti." Kunti looked at Ghatotkacha with a mix of disgust and sorrow. Mother and son prostrated to Kunti. "May you... be well. I bless you," said Kunti.

As Ghatotkacha and Hidimbi were going to leave, Kunti walked up to them. "Ghatotkacha, you will always be considered the first Pandava son." Ghatotkacha smiled at Kunti. "Thank you, Grandmother."

Ghatotkacha and Hidimbi made their way back into the deep forest. Bheema and the Pandavas looked on until they were out of sight.

Thus goes the story of Ghatotkacha's birth.

MARKETING: Ugly Timing!

Being Ugly...

Despite being ugly and people looking at him with suspicion, Ghatotkacha respects his mom and proceeds to move on. From the initial shock, he wins people over with his respect, and later on with his abilities. With time, there is the usual exaggeration about his size and capabilities. Episodes of his prowess get inflated! The accompanying marketing fluff positions him as a person with magical abilities to solve any problem!

What does that have to do with marketing?

Ugly products still become a hit (at times).

Ugly products are spoken about so much that people flock to the stores to buy them, thereby making the product trendy. At times, it is a deliberate marketing ploy. Such products are designed to go way against the norm and are priced in such a way that the combination becomes a significant talking point. This is a gamble, of course.

Take Crocs, for example. There have been quite some comments about the Croc look. People complain and comment on the ugliness. Yet, there is a growing section that likes the product's comfort and ease of use. They wear Crocs with pride, and advocate Crocs to their friends, leading to word of mouth and repeat sales.

In fact, Crocs ran an advertisement that claimed: "Ugly can be beautiful!"

A print ad for Volkswagen Beetle ran with the headline "Ugly is only skin deep." The ad started with the line "It may not be much to look at..." The customers answered with their wallets!

You've heard of movies so bad, you still watch them and talk about them. This makes them a cult hit! For example, *The Room* (2003), *Show Girls*, *Plan 9 from Outer Space*, *Narasimha* (Tamil).

TIMING – Knowing When to Appear

Concerning Krishna, the debate continues as to whether he is good or bad. Krishna is the ultimate strategic marketer. He demonstrates a very clear long-term vision and pointed tactics to achieve short- and long-term goals.

He is the *sutradhar* (the puppeteer), holding several threads and controlling each of them effectively. As we proceed with the book, we shall learn more about Krishna's strategies. He knew where to be when and what to say and do!

It's all about timing.

I launched an online survey company in 2000, eResearchIndia. I got the first database of people who could take a survey and launched the division. Newspaper coverage followed suit.

Business, however, fell flat as I was way ahead of the curve. Internet penetration in India was still minuscule. The online survey methodology did not hold muster on the grounds of sample representativeness. It was a question of timing and I had to bite hard and close that division.

I waited nine years and then restarted that initiative as I believed in the potential. It turned out to be a significant success in its second life! Timing and the need for macro and microenvironment awareness contributed to the success. These are key lessons that I learned as I went ahead and committed newer errors!

* * * * *

WIELD THE MACE:

What clear distinction will you create today for your company or solution?

The Meeting

Hidimbi was in the forest with her son Ghatotkatcha. Being an *asuri*, Hidimbi went back to her barbaric ways. Hidimbi did not eat humans, but she sacrificed them. One such day, they had no luck in finding a human. They had not seen a single human that day.

Suddenly, Hidimbi's eyes grew wide. She started to breathe faster. "Son, I think I smell someone. Go in that direction and see if you can get someone for our sacrifice." She pointed to the direction from where she got the smell and Ghatotkacha followed her command.

As he went, he saw that his mother was right. There was a family of four – a man, a woman and two small children. Ghatotkatcha presumed that they had lost their way in the forest. He reduced his size to that of a normal being and went to them. "My name is Ghatotkatcha. What are you doing in a forest in the night?"

The man, the head of the family, spoke. "We have lost our way. Could you give us directions to go out of here?"

"No, I cannot. But I am searching for a human who I am to sacrifice today. One of you will have to come with me." The man's eyes showed fear. His two short children, a girl and a boy, stepped forward. The woman, the mother, pushed the children back with stern eyes. The same woman spoke. "I will go." The man looked at her and shook his head. "No. The children may be able to survive without a father, but not without a mother. I will go."

The man stepped forward. As Ghatotkatcha was about to lead him away, another man appeared. "Who are you? Why are you taking this man away?"

"I am a *half-asura,* Ghatotkatcha. This man is to be my sacrifice."

"He is a man with a family. Have mercy on him."

"I need a human for my sacrifice."

"Then take me!" yelled the new man.

"It does not make a difference to me. Well then, come along. I cannot afford to be late." Ghatotkatcha led the stranger through the bushes. "What are you doing here? The family has lost their way. Have you too?"

The stranger took his time replying. "I was lost. I thought that I had found my way when I found the family." "Hmm..." replied Ghatotkatcha. "Why do you sacrifice people, Ghatotkacha?"

"My mother and I have been sacrificing people for a long time. We sacrifice them to please the Goddess Kali."

"Sacrificing people is wrong, Ghatotkacha. I suggest that you let me go and convince your mother that what she is doing is wrong."

"You dare tell me what is right and what is wrong? Remember, you are the one to be sacrificed. Let you go it seems!"

"Why don't we have a duel. If I win, you let me go. If I don't, you can sacrifice me, as per your original plans."

Ghatotkatcha was surprised by the man's courage and smiled. "I agree. But I must tell you, my true form is terrifying. It strikes fear into the hearts of whoever sees it. I also have unmatchable strength due to a boon. Think this over and tell me your answer."

"That does not matter. I also have a lot of strength. Come, let us duel."

Ghataotkatcha laughed. His laughter echoed across the forest. A few birds flew away. "Well then, let us duel indeed!" Ghatotkatcha grew in size and was almost of the same size as a small hill. He held his hand up and in his hand was a golden mace with elaborate carvings.

The man marvelled at the sight of the huge Ghatotkatcha. He then smiled and made the same gesture as Ghatotkatcha. In his hand also, he held a mace. The man's mace was not as elaborate as Ghatotkatcha's. "Do not think that you can win just because of your size. Size is not everything. If you think that becoming big will be a problem for me, think twice."

Ghatotkatcha returned the man's smile with a smirk. "Do you want me to make myself smaller? Will that be easier for you? Or shall I just admit defeat?" He laughed. "Fine then. I will make myself smaller." Ghatotkatcha reduced his height to that of the man's. "Enough talk. Let us duel."

They ran towards each other wielding their maces. They swung their maces at each other. Both the maces crashed against each other. It created such a terrifying sound that an entire flock of birds flew away, scared by the sound.

Meanwhile, Hidimbi worried. She knew that Ghatotkatcha would be able to take care of himself, but as a mother, she still worried. *Was this how Hidimbaa had felt all those years ago?* She then heard a deafening sound. Hidimbi could no longer wait around. She decided to go in search of Ghatotkatcha.

Back at the clearing, the two were still fighting. Both tried using tricks, but neither got an advantage over the other. Weary, they wondered if one of them would ever win. They picked up their maces to fight again when a lightning bolt struck. It struck the ground right between the two.

In place of the lightning bolt stood Hidimbi. When she saw Ghatotkatcha, she breathed a sigh of relief. "Ghatotkatcha! I have been waiting all this while for you! What have you been doing?"

"Mother, worry not. Our sacrifice wanted to duel with me. If he wins the duel, I will let him go. If I win, he will be sacrificed. The fight is still going on. Once we are done, I will come back home." Saying so, Ghatotkatcha picked up his mace.

Hidimbi turned around to look at the man who had challenged her son. Her eyes widened. She turned back to face Ghatotkatcha. "Ghatotkatcha! Stop fighting this instant! This man is no stranger. He is your father, Bheema!"

Ghatotkatcha stopped in his tracks. Tears came to his eyes. Both dropped their maces. They embraced each other. "Father, if you ever need anything, just think of me. I will come to you."

This is how Ghatotkacha met Bheema after many years.

MARKETING: Letting Go

Relating to the story, Bheema asked Ghatotkacha to let go of old practices, like human sacrifice. I am only taking two words from that conversation – letting go. Aren't we prisoners of old habits and customs? Should we not change with the times? What does letting go have to do with me or you as marketers?

What does it mean in a marketing context, today?

Letting Go

Letting go of mass marketing: Especially for startups, bootstrappers and those who want to do smart marketing, the focus and need is for niche marketing. The need is to identify a core target clientele and focus on bringing about positive change for this curated segment.

Letting go of the being-on-top position everywhere: *"Why do you need to be in the top 10 in the Wall Street Journal or The New York Times?"* This question was put forth to me by book coach Kiruba Shankar. This question took me by shock and then the reality set in. *Who am I writing for? Not the whole world!* I am not writing fiction. I write marketing books for a very specific target audience. Therefore, I am happy being a best seller in that specific segment! The whole world is NOT my market.

Product, product, feature, feature: We need to let go of the product/feature mentality to focus on the customer need, want, benefit and usage. They decide, they use, they buy again and they spread the word. Your solution fulfils a key requirement; how you best do that is all that counts.

Growth at all costs: This thought has to be replaced by **sustainable growth**. A focus on unit economics and growing from within is required today. Let us assume there is no possibility of external funding for your business; will you close shop then? Or will you focus on coming with a business plan that is self-sustaining so you can grow from within?

All are equal: That statement is a myth! All customers are not equal. Some customers love you. Some hate you and there are quite a few in the middle. You have to decide who is more valuable and who needs more quality time investment from you. For a new product or solution, who are those who are most likely to try you out, to embrace the new and to spread the word?

This is the way it has always been done: Is it? Well, not anymore. Let go! Dissect each of the strategies and tactics you employ to find out which one brings in revenue and which one meets and exceeds the original objective for which it was used. Go full-on KonMari* on your marketing tactics and throw away those that

---

*   The **KonMari method** is a system of simplifying and organizing your home by getting rid of physical items that do not bring joy into your life.

have not brought in returns in the last 6–12 months.
There's a need to do the right thing even when all odds
are stacked against you.

* * * * *

WIELD THE MACE:

**Which of your practices are you letting go of today?
Make a list. Act on it.**

The Mere Thought

The Pandavas were still in their period of exile. This involved a lot of walking. It was a hot day and there seemed to be no water anywhere.

After many hours of walking on foot, the exhausted brothers fell down. They could not move any further. They needed water immediately, but there seemed to be no water. Everyone was wondering what to do, as even a small exertion was too tiring. They were lying on the ground with the hard sun beating upon them without mercy.

When one is at the end of the tether, good memories of family and friends come to mind. Was it a hallucination or a sense of what was to come soon?

Bheema thought of Hidimbi and Ghatotkacha as he started sinking into a stupor.

As soon as Bheema thought of Ghatotkacha, he appeared immediately. Ghatotkacha looked at his unconscious uncles, grandmother and stepmother. Nobody could speak or respond; they could not even sense his presence. He knew what had happened and what needed to be done.

Smiling to himself, he carried the seven of them on his back. Being *half-asura,* he could carry enormous weights easily. He could also teleport himself to different locations. It is said that Ghatotkacha carried them to the Badryashrama or Badri hermitage. The hermitage is in Kedarnath, India.

Ghatotkacha ensured that they got enough water and rest. In a way, Ghatotkacha saved the Pandavas single-handedly!

MARKETING: You and Your Client

When the client thinks of a solution, whom does he think of?

> *"All things being equal, people will do business with, and refer business to, those people they know, like and trust."*
>
> – The Go-Giver, Bob Burg and
> John David Mann

You must serve your clients so well that they know you will be there for them when there is a need. You must do it with more thrust when your client is undergoing pain or a downturn.

Can you anticipate these needs and be there ahead of time?

Plan solutions for those who are yet to become your customers! Engage in future planning.

How will they come to you? They will come to you through the initial set of clients that you continue to wow.

How can you be top-of-the-mind for your clients? How do you make people aware of you and your solution?

Here is an example:

Krux108, my outlier marketing consulting entity, was developing a game. The purpose of the game was to introduce four key concepts of marketing to my clients and their associates. This was the first game from our stable and so considerable time was invested in it, with multiple rounds of playtests. For each playtest round, we invited entrepreneurs and marketers to play and share their feedback. The card game was played using our paper prints from our office printer, with the cards being cut manually. It was still in development testing mode.

For the fourth playtest, we invited Arun Ramkumar, a designer and the founder of Mojo Canvas, a design house. He played a couple of rounds and shared his set of suggestions and changes. This happened on a Saturday. The following Monday, I received an email from Arun. This email had an attachment with the full set of 52 cards designed with the framework and flow. He had coordinated with the game designer Kartic Vaidyanathan from Play2Learn and the game lead Jayalakshmi. He worked two days straight and sent across designs for the card game Majaaa.

Arun did not wait for a brief, purchase order or approval. He knew the cards had to be designed and he went ahead and did it.

When I think of design, I think of Arun and Mojo Canvas.

When I think of gamifying, I think of Kartic Vaidyanathan.

* * * * *

WIELD THE MACE:

What will you do consistently?
What makes your client think of you?

The War Brews

There was a war brewing in the country. The two protagonists of the war were the Pandavas and the Kauravas.

The Mahabharata is a compilation of stories that show us that no one is fully black (bad) or white (good). Everybody is grey; they are good and bad. In modern retellings of *The Mahabharata*, many characters are portrayed as entirely good or entirely bad. But, many incidents prove that they are only human.

The Pandavas and Kauravas were cousins. Their fathers, Pandu and Dhritarashtra, were brothers. They had another uncle called Vidura. Both parties were from the Chandravanshi or the Lunar dynasty. (In the *Ramayana*, we come across the Suryavanshi or the Solar dynasty.)

The war happened due to the enmity between the two families:

Duryodhana, the eldest Kaurava, and Yudhishtra, the eldest Pandava, were both fighting for the throne.

The Pandavas were five brothers and the sons of Pandu and Kunti. Although they had different fathers (and mothers), they were hailed as the sons of Pandu.

Yudhishtra was the first Pandava, son of Yama and Kunti.

Bheema was the second, son of Vayu and Kunti.

Arjuna was the third, son of Indra and Kunti.

Nakula and Sahadeva were twins, sons of the Ashwini twins and Madri.

The Kauravas were 100 sons. They had one sister. The main Kauravas were Duryodhana (the eldest son) and Dushasana (the second son). Dhritarashtra, the blind king, was their father and Queen Gandhari was their mother.

This chapter provides a background to the stories that follow.

MARKETING: Who is Good, Who is Bad?

Who is good and who is bad – only the situation will make that clear!

The same applies to your marketing plan and tactics. Just because one method did not work now, it does not mean that the method was wrong or may never work again. Build a long list of all these experiments and attempts, along with the situation and players therein. This outreach database will help future ideations.

What works now need not work at a different time or for a different situation.

Continuing from the previous paragraph, what works now, needn't work later. The playbook that served you well for two years will need to be updated, enhanced and adapted.

As the wind blows, people switch sides. How often and how effectively are you checking the pulse of the market?

Photography is my hobby and I shoot in the RAW format, which gives a greater leeway/range while editing. As a stress buster, I pick up images that I had clicked about 10 years ago and reprocess them. When I compare the edited versions of the same image, across the years, it is evident that each image output looks different. The base raw image remains the same but my interpretation has changed over the years.

I have evolved as a person and as an amateur photographer. Other influences leave an impact on my artistic outlook.

This is the case with your client as well.

What worked for them, then, needn't be the same now. The client has moved on to gain other experiences and enhanced needs.

Have you or your solution moved along with the times? Have you evolved?

Let us relate to the war now. There are pertinent questions to ask yourself and write it down. It may seem like a lot of questions, but your answers will make the path ahead clearer.

What are the next steps for you?

The war for market share? Or a war for survival? What are you looking at?

What is your objective with your business? Is it to gain market share and increase profitability? Or is it that you just want to survive a downturn and plan for another day? If it is a question of the survival of your business, then it is a war! Who forms a part of your team? Who forms a part of your extended army? Who are your mentors and strategists?

* * * * *

WIELD THE MACE:

Answer all the questions above and arrive at your strategic war map – your marketing plan!

MAYABAZAAR

The Imaginary Marketplace

MAYABAZAAR is an important episode in the life of Ghatotkacha. It has been covered in a lot of stories and super hit movies.

The episodes have been retold here as there is so much to know and learn.

The Prelude to a Marriage

Subhadra, the sister of Krishna and Balarama, was married to the Pandava Arjuna. She had a son with him named Abhimanyu. Balarama, the brother of Subhadra and Krishna, had a daughter by the name Sasirekha. She was also known as Vatsala. Abhimanyu fell in love with Sasirekha.

The Kauravas invited the Pandavas to play a game in their capital Hastinapur. The game was one of dice, traditionally called *Daayakattai*. The game, though, was a trick to rid the Pandavas of all their belongings.

Duryodhana had an uncle called Shakuni. Shakuni was the brother of Duryodhana's mother, Gandhari. Shakuni was the one who proposed the idea of tricking the Pandavas. Shakuni cunningly played the game in the Kauravas' favour. The Kauravas were successful in their endeavour. The Pandavas gambled and lost their palace, their wealth and even their wife, Draupadi.

They were banished to an exile period of 13 years. Dushasana, Duryodhana's brother, tried to disrobe

Draupadi post the game as the Kauravas claimed to have won her in the game. Lord Krishna came to her rescue, where no matter how much Dushasana tried, the cloth of her sari that covered her body never ended. Krishna was infuriated that the Kauravas tried to disrobe her. Balarama marched to Hastinapur when he heard about this.

Balarama went to confront the Kauravas. Duryodhana and Shakuni spoke to Balarama with respect. Duryodhana, in reality, wanted his son to marry Balarama's daughter. By doing so, Duryodhana believed that Balarama would support the Kauravas in the war.

Not aware of the initiative behind the proposal, Balarama agreed to the marriage. It was fixed, but...

who would marry whom?

MARKETING: A Calculated Risk!

GAMBLE AWAY if you must, but know your opponent. Do not let your ego get in the way.

It is easy to be swayed by others' words and our ego.

Who am I fighting with? What are his skills? Is this a game of equals?

Do I have the necessary skills or should I use a proxy if I decide to gamble?

When I know the field as best as I can, know the variables and then take a call, it is a calculated risk. When I shoot in the dark, relying only on prayers, **that is a gamble**.

A business is a game of calculated risks! One that we need to play to survive and succeed.

Consider the known risks, existing and potential, and plan out the possible outcomes and your action/reaction to it. Then decide whether it is a calculated risk.

In this way, you increase your odds of success and plan for the key skills to be brought in. You know that bad outcomes will happen during a project. With effective risk management, you anticipate what might happen, examine and prioritize these possible bad events and plan out what you will do about them.

When evaluating risks and options, "I don't know" is a perfectly fine answer, but our ego does not permit us to say that, even to ourselves.

It gets worse if you are a CEO or a marketer, as the rest of the team is looking up to you. Several initiatives have collapsed due to the small three-letter word, EGO.

Let us look at a real-life business example:

Michael Dublin smelled a new trend in the market, that of subscription boxes. Companies like Birchbox had successfully piloted sending cosmetic boxes with samples for their clientele. The box contained a mix of products, essentially lifestyle pieces that went together. Convenience and door-delivery with simple payment options – these were key reasons the subscription business was on the upswing.

What is there for men? What is their need and what is their want? These questions were rolling around in Michael's mind. *They need to shave and need all the accessories. Is there a market? Isn't it already crowded?*

He decided to take a calculated risk and based his moves on consumer behaviour.

In general, men don't like to look at multiple options and decide every time. What if Michael could do the same for men? He decided to take the guesswork out and deliver a pack at regular intervals.

Michael started the Dollar Shave Club. He packed his boxes with razors, blades, shaving cream and after-shave. He threw in a few optional grooming accessories. Michael got ready for a battle with the biggies dominating the men's grooming space!

He decided to shave off a segment of that market for his business!

By 2016, four years after the launch, the Dollar Shave Club secured over 50% of the online shaving market. Gillette made a belated move and launched its own subscription service but could not catch up with Dollar Shave Club.

* * * * *

WIELD THE MACE:

Which calculated risks are you considering today?

Success has many fathers.
Failure has one.
You!
Smile on, nevertheless

A Hate-Love Relationship

Krishna knew of Duryodhana's real intentions concerning the marriage proposal. He called his charioteer Daaruka. "Daaruka, take Subhadra and Abhimanyu to Ghatotkacha. Wait with them until further instructions arrive."

Daaruka, ever loyal to Krishna, took Abhimanyu and Subhadra to the forest.

"Mother, what are we doing here?" asked Abhimanyu.

Subhadra smiled. "Abhimanyu, my brother is smart. He would not have sent us here without reason. Daaruka, did Krishna say anything about the reason behind this trip?"

Daaruka shook his head and said sheepishly, "I do not know anything, princess. If Lord Krishna wanted me to tell you, he would have instructed me to do so."

Subhadra smiled. She observed the forest around her as Abhimanyu walked around. Abhimanyu let out an exclamation. "Mother! There is a house here. I think that Uncle Krishna meant for us to stay here."

The three entered the house. The house was as big as a small palace. They found no one inside and settled in. There were beds with cushions. The flashing colours were jarring against the walls, which had old paint peeling off. Subhadra and Abhimanyu rested while Daaruka stood outside.

Subhadra and Abhimanyu were talking and observing the house. It was well decorated but still simple. The house looked like the owner was expecting a guest. Subhadra and Abhimanyu assumed that Krishna had gotten it ready for them.

Suddenly, they heard cries. Daaruka ran in panting. "Princess Subhadra... Prince Abhimanyu! Get yourselves out of here!"

"Daaruka, calm down. What happened?"

Daaruka caught his breath and swallowed nervously. "Princess, it is-"

He was cut off as there was a tremor in the ground and a giant entered the house.

Abhimanyu and Subhadra stared in shock. Daaruka took a rod lying nearby and threw it at the giant. The giant started to laugh. "You think that you can match my skills with an iron rod?"

The giant kicked the rod. It rolled across the floor and stopped at Subhadra's feet.

"If you want to live, run away. I will give you ten minutes," said the giant.

"Listen, I am the sister of the Lord himself. So I suggest that you run away from here before I prove our prowess in combat," Subhadra challenged as she picked up the rod.

The giant laughed again. "You think that you can defeat me in my own house? And that too, of all people, a lady? You think a lady can defeat me?" The giant simply plucked the rod out of her hand.

Abhimanyu was enraged. *How dare he laugh at his mother?!* Abhimanyu closed his eyes and chanted. Lo, on his shoulders stood a quiver filled with arrows, and in his hand his bow*.

Abhimanyu looked at the giant with disgust. The giant smiled and pushed the three of them out of the house with one hand. "You just threw us out because you are scared of being defeated! If you have courage, come out and let us fight!" yelled Abhimanyu.

---

* Most characters in the *Mahabharata* have a special weapon with a distinct name. Abhimanyu's weapon was the same as his father, the bow and arrow. His bow was called Raudra.

"My skills are unmatchable. I do not want to hurt your pride, as you look like a royal. It might be bad for your image to know that you were beaten by a giant."

"Image, my foot! If you are not scared, fight me! I will win. No words are needed to tell me that you are a coward."

The giant glowered at the young prince. Then his eyebrows eased and he smiled. "If you want to..." Abhimanyu's eyes showed surprise when he saw that the giant wielded a mace.

"To make things fair, don't we have to fight with the same weapon?" asked Abhimanyu.

"These sound like excuses. What are you scared of if you think you are going to win?" taunted the giant.

Abhimanyu glared at the giant. He positioned himself and let an arrow fly. It went over the giant's left shoulder. Abhimanyu stared aghast. He had never missed a target. The giant swung his mace, but Abhimanyu was faster. He jumped higher than the mace and unleashed another arrow, directed at the giant's neck. The arrow hit its target and Abhimanyu smiled. But the giant did not show any signs of pain and swung the mace again.

The mace hit Abhimanyu's leg. Abhimanyu gave a startled cry and cursed himself for being stupid. One is simply stupid if he decides to be distracted while in a battle with someone of higher skill. Abhimanyu tried moving his leg and winced at the pain. This giant had strength!

But he decided to use his position to his advantage. He released an arrow that hit the giant right where his heart should have been. The giant smiled and simply pulled the arrow out. He flicked the tiny arrow into the trees and got ready to swing his mace.

Abhimanyu rolled over just as the mace hit the spot he was sitting on a few moments ago. "Listen, I am going easy on you. Or else, you would have more than a broken leg to worry about. I suggest that you go away before you bring yourself more injuries."

Abhimanyu's pride was hurt. He had always beaten his enemies with ease before. But this giant possessed inhuman strength. "I have always beaten my enemies... are you a god?" he asked.

The giant laughed, "No. I am Ghatotkacha, a *half-asura* and half man."

Abhimanyu's eyes widened in realization. "So you are the great Ghatotkacha! I have heard so many stories of you from Uncle Bheema!"

"Who are you? How do you know Bheema?"

"I am Abhimanyu. I am the son of Arjuna."

It was now Ghatotkacha's eyes that widened. "So you are my cousin, Abhimanyu! Krishna has informed me about you. He said that you would be in a chariot. When I saw you at my house, I thought that you were one of those Kauravas that my father had told me about."

"Me? A Kaurava? Never, Ghatotkacha!"

Ghatotkacha looked at Subhadra. She returned his curious gaze with a stare.

"Wait... that must make you-"

"Princess Subhadra, Abhimanyu's mother." She continued to stare at him with narrowed eyes."

"Mother Subhadra, I apologize for my behaviour. I did not know who you were." Ghatotkacha prostrated before Subhadra.

"Ghatotkacha, it is fine. I expect that even I would have done the same had I seen strangers in my house."

"Abhimanyu, your leg! Come, let us go into my house. I can tend to you there."

Ghatotkacha lifted Abhimanyu and brought him into the house. He laid Abhimanyu on a sofa and went to get water.

Subhadra sat on a seat next to Abhimanyu. "Mother, do you think that Uncle Krishna meant for us to meet Ghatotkacha?"

"I expect so. One can never guess what goes on in that mind of his. How are you feeling, Abhimanyu?"

"I am fine. He is even more powerful than what Uncle Bheema said! He is the best opponent that I have fought against!"

Subhadra smiled. Her son had the same attitude as his father, anger mixed with admiration.

Ghatotkacha returned with dark green leaves and some water. He applied the leaves on Abhimanyu's leg and poured the water on it. He raised his hand above it and Abhimanyu let out a scream.

"That will ensure that the bone grows back stronger and faster, " said Ghatotkacha.

"Did you know that we were to meet Ghatotkacha, Daaruka?" asked Subhadra. Daaruka nodded.

Krishna had not sent any word asking the mother and son to come back so Subhadra and Abhimanyu stayed with Ghatotkacha. Abhimanyu and Ghatotkacha became very close. Ghatotkacha showed Abhimanyu his magic and how to wield a mace. Abhimanyu showed Ghatotkacha different techniques in archery. Together, they were indestructible!

This was how the cousins met each other.

MARKETING: Lovers and Haters

Hate at first sight.

Love on the tenth!

Have you ever felt this?

Ghatotkacha fought with his father without knowing who he was. It was the same case with Abhimanyu. The hate-fight could have ended differently.

Hate

You hate something or someone from the first sight or interaction. You don't know why but something is off! You move on but you keep bumping into that person as you share common social circles. It starts with a small smile of recognition when you meet and progresses to awkward conversations. As the interactions increase, you get more comfortable and as you get to know that person more, you begin to like that person. The liking turns into friendship and at times, love!

Have you felt it with a product? Something that you didn't quite like at first, either because it was not good or you were being forced to use it. This enforced usage exhibited itself as hate. As you kept using the product, you found that it solved quite a lot of your problems. You got used to the product and before you knew it, it became an integral part of your life. Something you cannot be without!

So what exactly do these two words mean?

Hate: intense dislike to the point of doing something bad.

Love: Caring; happiness in others' happiness; realizing that each person is unique and therefore capable of achieving and doing a lot of things.

When you show genuine interest in the well-being of a person, hate slowly slips away, leaving care, hope and love in its wake.

Customer relationships can be salvaged. Users can be made to like. Likers can be given a unique experience to make them lovers!

Be wary though, for it takes a long time to get love into the equation but just one slip for hate to emerge.

How can you convert your haters into likers, or better still, your superfans?

- Invest time.

- Researching the problem: Is it a genuine problem or concern? If yes, resolve and keep the communication on.

- There will always be some haters who cannot be convinced. It is necessary to identify who they are. Perhaps this solution is not for them. Or they are like that only! Find out the decision-making unit, who influences, who decides, who buys and who uses your solution. This has to be done for B2C or for B2B, based on your solution. If it is a B2B user base, then the product (solution) usage could have been forced from top-down; hence some people may be rebelling. This may actually have nothing to do with the quality of your solution! Involve the whole decision-making unit when the testing/buying process is on. Encourage people to speak directly to you.

- Look at your top 10% of clients, especially those who are vocal about positive reviews. They have used your solution, they care and they spread the word. If they have mentioned comments online, I am certain they will be talking about you to their friends and connections as well. This is positive word of mouth. They are already your superfans. They are the best persons to talk to some of the haters.

- For the rest, talk to them in their voice. Match their background and way of communicating.

- Involve them in your plans, tests and actions. Make them insiders and a part of you/your company.

- Show genuine care and concern. Keep the communication on and personalize the interactions.

- Say thanks, in as many unique ways you can think of.

* * * * *

WIELD THE MACE

Identify who your haters and lovers are!

Anger is not the Answer

Subhadra, Abhimanyu, Hidimbi and Ghatotkacha were sitting in Ghatotkacha's house. Subhadra and Abhimanyu met Hidimbi in the morning. It was afternoon, and the sunlight spilt into the house through the huge windows and doors.

"Is there any particular reason that you are here, Mother Subhadra? I have been wanting to ask you, " asked Ghatotkacha.

"Daaruka, would you care to explain?"

"Princess Subhadra, Lord Krishna has sent you to be with Ghatotkacha for a reason. Lord Balarama has agreed to the marriage of Sasirekha and Lakshmana Kumara. Lakshmana Kumara is the son of Duryodhana."

"Is uncle Balarama not aware of the Kauravas' crooked ways?" exclaimed Abhimanyu. "Why have they organized the marriage, Daaruka?"

"The Kauravas have planned the marriage to have Lord Balarama's support in the war."

Hearing this, Ghatotkacha became angry. "How dare those Kauravas do this? Have they no shame? They are begging for support. And Balarama! He must be blind to the intentions of the Kauravas. I will go and wage war against those sleazy dogs!"

Hidimbi walked up to Ghatotkacha. She sat beside him and placed her hand on his shoulder. "Ghatotkacha, not everything requires a war. There are different solutions to different problems."

Ghatotkacha let out a sigh. His anger was like his father, Bheema's. "I expect that Krishna wants your help in disrupting the wedding, but in a different way. Why don't you use your magic? It is as good as mine," counselled Hidimbi.

"Mother, that is a good idea. I will start now. I will bring Sasirekha here. It is a long trip to Dwaraka. Take care of Abhimanyu and Princess Subhadra!" Saying so, he flew into the blue sky with his mace.

MARKETING: The Alternatives

When Ghatotkacha hears the predicament of Abhimanyu, he immediately wants to rush into battle. It does not take much time for his blood to boil and for him to jump into action. *I need to do something right away!* This rage can be equated with an entrepreneur's mindset of getting things done – The initial euphoria of a brilliant idea and the need to execute it immediately, lest it goes up in smoke over time!

Yes, speed is necessary and we need to strike when the iron is hot – but only after we evaluate the options and what needs to be done.

Once the objective is clear, then we must plan our next course of action. In the story, it was to teach Duryodhana and his clan a lesson while getting Abhimanyu married to Sasirekha.

Was war the only option?

Hidambi stepped in and asked Ghatotkacha to use his magical powers. He decides to do so and sneak Sasirekha out from her palace!

There are always alternative ways to achieve the set objective.

Each of us has unique experiences and specific skill sets. We have an existing network with its connections, access to specific know-how and the landscape (not literally. I mean the technology, or the industry environment).

Get outside help when and where required.

The best idea does not exist in a vacuum. There are others who have solved the same or similar problem. Why did they do? How did they solve or meet the objective? Idea combination works here as well.

Looking back at the Dollar Shave Club example

Michael Dublin knew that fighting Gilette and the shaving market in the traditional battleground was a losing situation. Instead, he chose a growing but untapped market of online ordering and a subscription box business model. He carved a niche here with his wacky video ads and outreach. He chose an alternative path.

* * * * *

WIELD THE MACE:

What are the strengths you already possess that will help you meet your objective effectively and in time?

Write it down. What do you have? Who do you know who can help?

Connect the dots.
Execute.
Measure.
Redo.
That's the outlier marketer's way to achievement.

The Kidnapping!

At Dwaraka, Krishna knew of Ghatotkacha's plan. He informed Sasirekha's attendants about Ghatotkacha's arrival. "There will be a giant that will come here and take away Sasirekha. Allow him to. Do not speak of this to anybody." The maids nodded their heads and went into their quarters.

Ghatotkacha reached Dwaraka the next day, a little past midnight. He reached a window and made sure that no one saw him. As he entered the room through the window, he saw Sasirekha sleeping and a maid watching over her.

"Who are you?" the servant-maid asked.

"Is this Princess Sasirekha?" Ghatotkacha asked. The servant-maid opened her mouth to answer but stopped herself. "If you don't tell me who you are, I will scream," she threatened.

"Please don't. I am here for Princess Sasirekha."

The servant-maid started to scream, but Ghatotkacha rushed in. He clamped her mouth shut with her hand. "Do not scream. I am Ghatotkacha. I trust that Krishna must have told you something?"

The servant nodded. "Okay." He removed his hands and pointed his finger at a lady sleeping on the bed, "Is she Princess Sasirekha?" The maid nodded.

Ghatotkacha lifted the sleeping princess and placed her on his back. He flew out from the window without another word.

He reached his house in the forest. The princess was still fast asleep, unaware of anything going on in her surroundings. Ghatotkacha brought her inside. The moment he put her on the sofa, Sasirekha woke up.

"Where am I? Who are you? Why did you bring me here?" she asked Ghatotkacha with a look of disgust. "You are at my house in the forest. I am Ghatotkacha. I am here to get you married to my cousin Abhimanyu."

"But my wedding-"

"Is tomorrow."

"And what about my parents? Do they know that I am gone?"

"But you are not gone. At least, the 'fake' you is not gone. You are still sleeping in your quarters."

"How?" Sasirekha asked.

"I can make copies of myself. I can also transform myself. So, my copy in the form of you is sleeping in Dwaraka.

"I cannot believe this! It is too good to be true! I did not want to marry that prince Lakshmana Kumara." Saying so, Sasirekha smiled at Ghatotkacha. "Thank you, Ghatotkacha."

"It is not me that you should thank. It is your uncle, Krishna."

MARKETING: Can You Clone Yourself?

As an entrepreneur and marketer, I am sure you've said this statement to yourself quite a few times; **If only I could clone myself!**

If only I had the powers of a Ghatotkacha, to transform at will and achieve my objective. If only....

Maybe not, but there are alternatives!

I have this feeling: "There is nobody who can do this job as well as I can do." Accept it. You've said that to yourself, many times. You are a control freak and need to be on top of everything happening in your company or division.

For me, the only way to clone myself, near enough, is to put in place a team and process that translates what needs to be done and executes it. This "process" needs to be written leaving not much scope for misinterpretation but enough to enable individual decision-making.

I received a lot of help in my career to get me where I am today. I need to ensure that the "to-be-cloned" team gets similar assistance and freedom and uses the power of automation.

Another way to ask this question is from a marketing perspective: How can I enable growth across channels whereby I can enable multiple sales at the same time? How can I provide the same service to a larger number of clients with the same core team that I have? Here are some suggestions:

- Assemble the right team, preferably scrappy individuals who will get things done.

- Find out what drives each of them and plan accordingly.

- Prepare this team to take effective leadership decisions and own them.

- Give them direction, but the freedom to learn it their way.

- Mutually set targets and strategies, giving them total tactical freedom.

- Get them to develop the next level team.

Each clone brings about quite a bit of individuality to the mix. Meeting/exceeding the objective should be the key goal.

Me as Ghatokacha: Well, I am planning for more digital assets and solutions, so I can fly more often wherever I want to go as my clones will keep the fires burning.

* * * * *

WIELD THE MACE:

What is your plan for cloning?

The Real Imaginary Place!

Ghatotkacha left Sasirekha at his house and flew back to Dwaraka.

Assuming the image of Sasirekha, Ghatotkacha slept on the bed. Ghatotkacha (as Sasirekha) then travelled to Hastinapur, the capital, along with Sasirekha's parents and Krishna.

The bride's side of the family reached Hastinapur in no time. Ghatotkacha, still in the form of Sasirekha, created a magical marketplace called Mayabazaar. *Maya* means illusion and *bazaar* means a market.

"I have heard that there is a new place called Mayabazaar. Why don't we perform the wedding of Sasirekha and Lakshmana Kumara there? I can have everything arranged," said Krishna.

The Kauravas were surprised, as Krishna never supported any of their actions. On Krishna's suggestion, the Kauravas went to Mayabazaar for the wedding. They reached and found the place too good to be true.

There was a palace which was festively decorated. It had plenty of space for both the groom's and the bride's side. Everyone was in a festive mood, enjoying the new changes in the environment. Duryodhana smiled along with his uncle, Shakuni. Everything was going according to plan. Happy that their plan was going well, Duryodhana walked around offering sweets.

In the meantime, Ghatotkacha performed the actual wedding of Sasirekha and Abhimanyu in his house. (Remember, he can multiply himself. So, he was in his house as well as in Mayabazaar.)

He took Sasirekha's place in the marriage of Sasirekha and Lakshmana Kumara. Krishna also cloned himself to attend the wedding of Sasirekha and Abhimanyu. (Krishna also has the power to clone himself.)

Back in Mayabazaar, one of Arjuna's disciples called Satyaki was present. "Prince Shakuni, why don't you stand on this?" he asked while helping Shakuni stand on a box that was present. The box was, though unknown to the onlookers, enchanted with magical spells. It forced Shakuni to tell the truth.

"Duryodhana and I wanted this marriage to happen. We organized it to have Balarama's support during the war."

When the truth was revealed, Ghatotkacha assumed his actual form. Balarama and the others stared in shock.

Shakuni then accused Krishna of sabotaging the wedding. "Krishna! Did you not plan this? I do not need an answer, because I know of your ways. You did this to spoil the name of the Kauravas!"

Krishna only smiled. "Shakuni, for everything that happens, you cannot blame me. If even a feather falls on your shoulder, you blame me for it. It is pointless trying to debate with you. You can accuse me of anything you like," he finished and smiled once more.

All the Kauravas were humiliated and they started their journey back to Hastinapur.

"You always get what you want, don't you, brother?" asked Balarama.

"Balarama, you never understand what you are getting yourself into. I was simply intervening where it was necessary. Meanwhile, your daughter is happily married to Abhimanyu."

Balarama and Revati (Sasirekha's mother) soon came to accept their daughter's marriage in the end.

This was how Ghatotkacha contributed to the marriage of Abhimanyu and Sasirekha. There is a popular Indian movie on this entire section titled *Mayabazar*.

MARKETING: Breaking the Objective and the Truth Box

Ghatotkacha broke the objective into multiple parts.

1. He got the bride out of the palace.

2. He moved her to a safe location.

3. Then went back and executed a series of steps towards the original objective.

The objective, or problem, can and must be broken down into smaller bits. It is easier to solve and a lot more fun to work this way.

He avoided the problem of conflict and bloodshed by using a different approach.

Okay, if this sounds simplistic, it is; as it should be! We cannot live with the simple, so we layer it with complexities and tie ourselves down in acting busy!

By breaking things down, we keep it simple!

The Truth Box:

Is it working? Are you achieving your objectives? Are you making money? Is your business generating the ROI you had planned for? Well, do you have a marketing plan?

In the story, Satyaki had a truth box! Where is yours?

Your personal truth box will answer these questions. The truth box is an analogy. Who, apart from yourself, holds you accountable? Do you have an internal audit team? A board of advisers?

To me, that is quite important. As entrepreneurs and marketers, we tend to get carried away with the next new shiny idea. At times, we forget to ask ourselves: "Is it working?" It is for this reason we need to establish our own truth box.

Demystify, from within and externally.

* * * * *

WIELD THE MACE:

Build your own accountability team

The Chakravyuham

Prince Abhimanyu is said to be an incarnation of the moon god Chandra's son.

It is said that Chandra did not want to be away from his son for long. "My son can only incarnate as Abhimanyu for 16 years. I cannot live without him longer," stated Chandra. Brahma, the god of creation, agreed to the condition. "Let it be so." This is believed to be the reason behind Abhimanyu living for 16 years[*].

Arjuna would narrate stories to his wife Subhadra when she was pregnant. On some days, he would narrate the different types of formations in war. People believe that the baby Abhimanyu heard and registered this information.

One such formation that Arjuna talked about was the Chakravyuham or wheel formation. Arjuna explained how to penetrate such a formation. When he looked at

---

[*] Some people believe that Abhimanyu was born earlier and died at 33 years of age. It is most commonly believed that he died at 16.

Subhadra, she was fast asleep. Not wanting to disturb her, he left the room without narrating how to get out of the Chakravyuham.

Other retellings say that Arjuna did indeed narrate the information. These stories say that since Subhadra was asleep, the baby did not hear Arjuna.

Later, when the Kurukshetra War had started, Abhimanyu was old enough to take part in it. He fought bravely against the older Kaurava soldiers. On the 13th day of the war, the Kauravas adopted the Chakravyuham as a defence. They did so on the orders of their wise commander-general, Drona.

There were only two people who knew how to enter and exit a Chakravyuham: Arjuna and Krishna. The Kauravas kept both of them engaged, not giving them a chance to enter the formation and destroy it.

From his father's narration, Abhimanyu knew how to enter the Chakravyuham formation. He did not know how to come out of it but knew that there would be no Pandava army left if the Chakravyuham was left alone. Bravely, Abhimanyu penetrated the formation.

Abhimanyu entered the formation with ease. At once, he found himself surrounded by his uncles and their army. The other Pandavas soon came to know about Abhimanyu and tried to enter the formation.

Jayadratha, the brother-in-law of Duryodhana, saw the Pandavas. He distracted them and made sure that they could not enter the formation.

As Jayadratha kept the Pandavas engaged, the other Kauravas closed in on Abhimanyu. Abhimanyu fought on undeterred. He had with him his bow, Raudra. With it, he killed Shakuni's brother Kalakeya. And then came Karna.

Karna was a skilled archer but lost to Abhimanyu four times successively. The first time, Abhimanyu shot at him repeatedly, not giving Karna time to retaliate. The second time Karna managed to injure Abhimanyu, but not fatally. The third time Abhimanyu shot Karna's quiver, and all of Karna's arrows littered the ground. Finally, the fourth time, Abhimanyu shot Karna in the arm while he was collecting his arrows.

Abhimanyu did not kill Karna but weakened him. He did this because Arjuna had sworn to kill Karna. The now tired Abhimanyu looked up to see Ghatotkacha busy with his own fight.

On Duryodhana's orders, Karna broke Abhimanyu's bow Raudra from the back. Abhimanyu picked up a chariot wheel laying on the ground and tried to defend himself with that. Kripa, one of the soldiers in the Kaurava army, cut the wheel in half. After that, the Kauravas kept attacking the unarmed Abhimanyu. Abhimanyu's body was pierced with many arrows.

As he fell, he saw Ghatotkacha staring at him from a distance, his face full of sorrow.

This story is not about Ghatotkacha. However, it is one that teaches an important lesson in the field of marketing.

The Chakravyuham

MARKETING: Chakravyuham Formation

The Chakravyuham is a military formation similar to a maze. The enemies are allowed to enter but are then trapped, surrounded and attacked from all sides. There is a specific strategy to penetrate and get out of a Chakravyuham. Those who do not know it die a violent death, as did Abhimanyu!

When you enter into a business, you should have a marketing strategy that is fully thought out. Without a strategy or an exit plan, the competition, or the economy or a combination thereof will crush you.

What are you getting into? What do you know about the environment, the clients and the competition? If not all, you need to know it, at least in parts.

Any business is like a Chakravyuham.

When you make your growth plans, you also need to do scenario planning.

Scenario planning is not a forecasting method as to what happens in the future.

It is about being prepared for whatever happens in the future!

Let us say you are planning for the future and want to bet big. The economy seems to be tanking.

Under the possible economic scenarios mentioned below, how am I planning today?

There are four possible scenarios denoted by the alphabets V, U, W and L. This is because the shape of the market recovery curve resembles the respective alphabet!

V:

Markets and demand tank all of a sudden but there will be an equally sharp uptick. I use the downtime to plan the processes, build prototypes and test the market. I ensure I have a good go-to-market strategy to implement as soon as I sense the upswing. I work on my existing connections and keep them warm and involved.

U:

There's a fall and the market takes some time to rise after the plateau at the bottom. I employ the same strategy mentioned above, except I design a few solutions that will keep my engine running during the plateau. I set price points at that level to suit the client need, to build relationships and explore areas of upset in the near future.

W:

The economy goes up and down and it will take time to get back to the original levels. I forget multi-year plans and do a quarter-by-quarter plan, with a severe grip on cash conservation and expense optimization. Each person in the team has to deliver more than their weight! This will be a crazy roller coaster and so one must keep the first-aid kit ready as there will be blood!

L:

This is the worst-case scenario where the entire market and demand tanks, not just for my solutions but globally. In such a scenario, I shift to major survival mode and work with a bare-bones core team. The purpose is to get ready for the new normal, which means that we need to deliver newer solutions for newer needs at a completely different and lesser price point. The solution and delivery model must take a drastic shift. I identify which parts of my solution portfolio need to be dropped. How do I survive first, then succeed in this new normal? Those are the answers I will find and implement, aggressively and at a fast clip.

I have friends and connections in the industry but each of them is busy in their own war for survival and embroiled in their own scenarios.

This is the Chakravyuham L scenario that I am currently planning for in detail.

* * * * *

WIELD THE MACE:

Get down and make your scenario plan today.
Be ready for all (planned) surprises!

The Inflection Point

Abhimanyu was killed unjustly during the Kurukshetra War on the 13th day of the war. Furious, Arjuna killed Jayadratha on the 14th day of the war. He did so because Jayadratha prevented the Pandavas from going to help Abhimanyu.

Duryodhana was enraged. "How dare he kill Jayadratha?! My sister Dhushala is distraught after learning about her husband's death. She has donned the clothes of a widow (white clothes) and has not eaten in days. She looks like a ghost!"

Karna said, "Duryodhana, there is not much that we can do. A person is bound to die in a war. Dhushala will get over it at some point. Just give her some time."

"Nothing we can do about it? Of course, we can do something about it! You, Karna, are going to kill Ghatotkacha, son of Bheema. That wretch of a giant deserves to die as compensation for Jayadratha. Anyways, he is our biggest threat now."

"But Duryodhana, how can I kill him? I have prowess in archery, but Ghatotkacha is a giant! He also possesses magical powers! It is impossible for me to kill such a being!"

"Karna, it is not impossible. You own the Vasava Shakthi, don't you? Use it against him. Why not go and kill him now? You know where the Pandava camp is. Use it, kill him and help me avenge Jayadratha."

Karna wanted to say something else, but Duryodhana's grief-stricken face quelled his misgivings. Duryodhana was his best friend, and Karna had never seen him so desolate. He wanted to save the Vasava Shakthi, a weapon from Indra, to kill Arjuna, his arch-enemy. The weapon was also referred to as the Indra Astra*.

Traditionally, a war ends at sunset. The war would continue at dawn the next day. It was forbidden to continue a war at night, and those that did so were considered cheats.

Although Karna was aware of the rule, he entered the Pandava camp close to midnight. He entered the camp with the intention of making Duryodhana happy.

---

* An Astra is a weapon with special powers, and is usually owned by a god. Indra is the God of lightning. He gave Karna the weapon after experiencing his kindness.

But what Karna did not know was that *asuras* grow more powerful during the night. He also did not know that Ghatotkacha had overheard them and he was ready for Karna.

Karna arrived at Ghatotkacha's tent, only to find him waiting. "Come to kill me, have you now, Karna?"

Karna's eyes flickered with fear. He masked it with a brave voice. "Yes, Ghatotkacha."

"You do know that it is against the rules to fight in the night-time?"

"I am well aware."

"Well then, what stops you? Shoot away."

Saying so, Ghatotkacha extended his arms. Karna was confused but shot his arrows one after the other. He did so until his quiver was empty.

Ghatotkacha laughed. "Do you think that shooting a few dozen arrows will kill me? I am *half-asura,* remember? I grow stronger during the night-time. Even normally, arrows will not be able to kill me."

Ghatotkacha held his hand out and there appeared his mace. Karna stared in awe. How could he have overlooked the fact that Ghatotkacha would be stronger in the night?!

Ghatotkacha only took one swing of his mace. It was enough to knock Karna out for a few seconds.

Ghatotkacha swung it again, and Karna landed many steps away. "Karna, it is late. I suggest that you go home." Saying so, Ghatotkacha entered the tent.

Karna, humiliated, walked back slowly to the Kaurava camp. It was almost dawn now, and Karna waited for the conch to blow, signalling the day's war.

Checking his armour, Karna picked up his bow and quiver. "Ghatotkacha, beware." Saying so, Karna made a little prayer to his father, the Sun God Surya.

Karna wandered the battlefield. He battled many soldiers, but only had Ghatotkacha on his mind. He searched for Ghatotkacha, but in vain. It was only around noon that he spotted Ghatotkacha.

"Finally! I have been searching for you all morning!" yelled Karna.

"Really? I'm flattered, Karna!" Ghatotkacha shouted over the cries of the ongoing battle.

"Listen here! I am going to defeat you, here and now! So you better not run off like a coward!"

"Karna, I assure you, I will not go anywhere. Especially after you wasted your time searching for me!" Ghatotkacha laughed. "I wonder who the coward is here, Karna!"

"I assure you, Ghatotkacha, it is you!"

"Well, let us fight again! I presume that is the reason behind your search?"

"No, Ghatotkacha, you big oaf! I searched for you so that I can give you sweets! Karna mocked. "Come, let us fight."

"Of course," replied Ghatotkacha. Karna released an arrow. Ghatotkacha caught it with two fingers and snapped it in half. "Karna, have you honestly learned nothing after yesterday? Pity. I pegged you for a quick learner, apparently not."

Ghatotkacha performed his signature move of holding his hand out. His mace appeared in his hand. Karna's mind replayed the previous day's fight. He swallowed nervously. Ghatotkacha swung his mace. Karna was ready for it. He moved a step. But what surprised him was that Ghatotkacha had expected this.

Karna's let out a scream as the mace hit his stomach. He had no words, but the food he had had in the morning was definitely coming back up.

"You look sick," Ghatotkacha laughed. "Face it, Karna, you've not got it in you. Go away while you have the chance."

Karna felt a dip in his confidence but changed his mindset. He remembered Duryodhana's face and made up his mind. He would not sleep unless he killed Ghatotkacha.

He picked up his bow once again and shot a series of arrows at Ghatotkacha. He then brought out his Vasava Shakthi. "Oh, bringing out the big toys, I see!"

Ghatotkacha multiplied himself just as Karna aimed the weapon at him. "Can you find me?" Ghatotkacha's voice echoed around Karna. Panic spread inside of Karna. He had, once again (for the nth time), underestimated Ghatotkacha and his abilities.

Karna then saw a ray of light. His father might be able to help him! Karna prayed fervently to his father, Surya. All of a sudden, Ghatotkacha's fake forms fell away, and only the true Ghatotkacha stood. Ghatotkacha increased his size but was too slow.

Not wasting a single moment, Karna unleashed the Vasava Shakthi. It hit Ghatotkacha, who died almost immediately. Even as he fell, he killed Kaurava soldiers. He is said to have killed an *Akshauhini*, or a formation of 21,780 chariots.

Seeing this, Lord Krishna smiled. He smiled because the Kauravas had used their most powerful weapon. Without the weapon, the Pandavas were in a situation that they could use to their advantage. The war was tilting in favour of the Pandavas. Would they use it to win?

This particular episode was the strategic inflection point in the Mahabharata war.

MARKETING: Growth by a 1000 Cuts!

When to make a move and why?

Do not move in without assessing the strengths and weaknesses of the enemy or the market.

With entrenched players, it is better to use a tactic other than direct confrontation.

What if you could keep chipping away at a section of existing users? What if you could build a true fan base of a 1000 followers who double up as your word of mouth sales ambassadors? (hat tip to Kevin Kelly). This is what I would call, **growth by a 1000 positive cuts.**

While you are doing this, you bring the competition into your strength area and do not go fight in theirs.

When it is your territory, you can then embark on a variation of death by a 1000 cuts. Be small and nimble and create enough small business entries, each of which makes a dent in the market share or operations of the competition. They are left to fight it out on multiple fronts while you continue to chip away, growing the business one fan at a time.

The competition will then be forced to use their best assets and resources to solve these small cuts, rather than focus on growth. They tend to get defensive while you continue to be on the incremental offensive. Their strength is then mitigated and the focus distorted.

You use a "Krishna" to be the master strategist who knows where to be and what to do. You use someone like a "Ghatotkacha" to be a significant tactical player creating havoc in the competitor's environment and mind.

Create a potential positive **inflection point** in the industry you work in (new clients, investment, growth). From that point on, your upward curve zooms and you need to plan for this change, while being wary of the next newcomer who will adopt the same strategies you did!

* * * * *

Bibliography

Historical references:

https://www.mahabharataonline.com/stories/mahabharata_character.php?id=70

http://www.blush.me/unwind/Ghatotkachas-mother-hidimbi-asura-father-bhima-pandava

https://en.wikipedia.org/wiki/Mayabazar

http://www.manuscrypts.com/myth/2012/02/28/ghatotkacha/

https://www.templepurohit.com/ghatotkacha-bhimas-son-and-the-rescuer-of-the-pandavas/

Marketing references:

https://www.cbc.ca/radio/undertheinfluence/selling-ugly-1.2912698 (Crocs ad)

https://www.businessinsider.in/retail/apparel/shoppers-are-dropping-hundreds-of-dollars-on-things-that-used-to-be-considered-too-ugly-to-wear-

here-are-the-worst-examples/articleshow/62903497.
cms

http://www.artfulthinkers.com/letting-go-of-old-
school-business

https://www.martechadvisor.com/articles/ux-and-
cro/5-marketing-practices-to-kill-in-2017/

https://hbr.org/1986/09/letting-go

Other Books by the Authors

Other Books by Pravin:

Other Books by Shraddha:

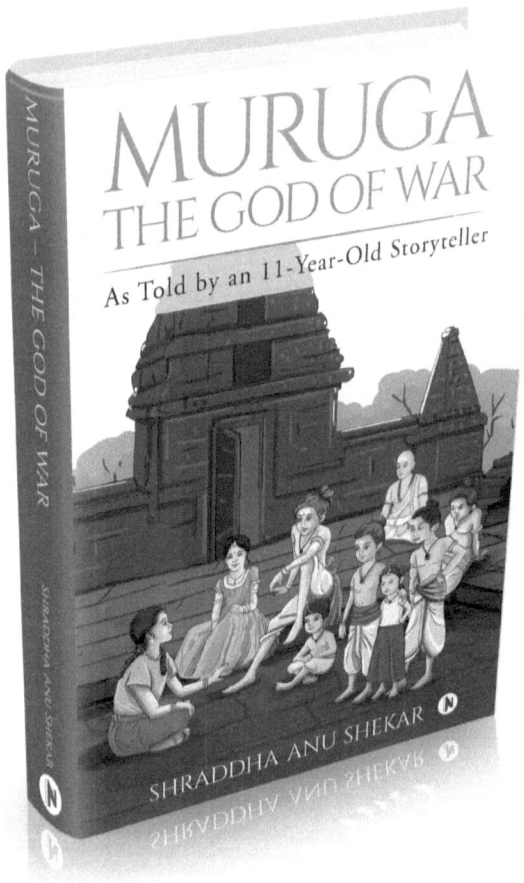

SHALYA

Stories from the
Mahabharatha

SHRADDHA ANU SHEKAR
The Teen Mythologist

www.ingramcontent.com/pod-product-compliance
Lightning Source LLC
Chambersburg PA
CBHW030718220526
45463CB00005B/2094